JavaScript
Pocket Reference

JavaScript
Pocket Reference

David Flanagan

Beijing • Cambridge • Farnham • Köln • Paris • Sebastopol • Taipei • Tokyo

JavaScript Pocket Reference

by David Flanagan

Copyright © 1998 O'Reilly & Associates, Inc. All rights reserved.
Printed in the United States of America. Published by O'Reilly &
Associates, Inc., 101 Morris Street, Sebastopol, CA 95472.

Editor: Paula Ferguson

Special Editions Editor: Gigi Estabrook

Production Editor: Paula Carroll

Production Services: Omegatype

Cover Design: Edie Freedman and Kathleen Wilson

Printing History:

October 1998:   First Edition

ISBN: 1-56592-521-1   [12/00]
[C]

Table of Contents

Versions of JavaScript 1

JavaScript Syntax 1

Variables 3

Data Types 4

Expressions and Operators.. 9

Statements 11

Regular Expressions.. 16

JavaScript in HTML 17

Client-side Object Hierarchy 19

Windows and Frames 19

Forms... 20

Events 21

JavaScript Security Restrictions... 21

Global Properties 24

Global Functions... 24

Alphabetical Object Reference 25

JavaScript
Pocket Reference

Versions of JavaScript

The following table specifies what versions of client-side JavaScript are supported by various versions of Netscape Navigator and Microsoft Internet Explorer:

Version	Navigator	Internet Explorer
2	JavaScript 1.0	
3	JavaScript 1.1	JavaScript 1.0
4	JavaScript 1.2; not fully ECMA-262 compliant prior to version 4.5	JavaScript 1.2; EMCA-262 compliant

JavaScript Syntax

JavaScript syntax is modeled on Java syntax, Java syntax, in turn, is modeled on C and C++ syntax. Therefore, C, C++, and Java programmers should find that JavaScript syntax is comfortably familiar.

Case sensitivity

JavaScript is a case-sensitive language. All keywords are in lowercase. All variables, function names, and other identifiers must be typed with a consistent capitalization.

Whitespace

JavaScript ignores whitespace between tokens. You may use spaces, tabs, and newlines to format and indent your code in a readable fashion.

Semicolons

JavaScript statements are terminated by semicolons. When a statement is followed by a newline, however, the terminating semicolon may be omitted. Note that this places a restriction on where you may legally break lines in your JavaScript programs: you may not break a statement across two lines if the first line can be a complete legal statement on its own.

Comments

JavaScript supports both C and C++ comments. Any amount of text, on one or more lines, between /* and */ is a comment, and is ignored by JavaScript. Also, any text between // and the end of the current line is a comment, and is ignored. Examples:

```
// This is a single-line, C++-style comment.
/*
 * This is a multi-line, C-style comment.
 * Here is the second line.
 */
/* Another comment. */ // This too.
```

Identifiers

Variable, function, and label names are JavaScript *identifiers*. Identifiers are composed of any number of ASCII letters and digits, and the underscore (_) and dollar sign ($) characters. The first character of an identifier must not be a digit, however, and the $ character is not allowed in identifiers in JavaScript 1.0. The following are legal identifiers:

```
i
my_variable_name
v13
$str
```

Keywords

The following keywords are part of the JavaScript language, and have special meaning to the JavaScript interpreter. Therefore, they may not be used as identifiers:

```
break          for            this
case           function       true
continue       if             typeof
default        import         var
delete         in             void
do             new            while
else           null           with
export         return
false          switch
```

In addition, JavaScript reserves the following words for possible future extensions. You may not use any of these words as identifiers either:

```
catch          enum           super
class          extends        throw
const          finally        try
debugger
```

Variables

Variables are declared, and optionally initialized, with the `var` statement:

```
var i;
var j = 1+2+3;
var k,l,m,n;
var x = 3, message = 'hello world';
```

Variable declarations in top-level JavaScript code may be omitted, but they are required to declare local variables within the body of a function.

JavaScript variables are *untyped:* they can contain values of any data type.

Global variables in JavaScript are implemented as properties of a special global object. Local variables within functions are implemented as properties of the Argument object for that function.

Data Types

JavaScript supports three primitive data types: numbers, boolean values, and strings. In addition, it supports two compound data types: object and arrays. Functions are also a first class data type in JavaScript, and JavaScript 1.2 adds support for regular expressions (described later) as a specialized type of object.

Numbers

Numbers in JavaScript are represented in 64-bit floating-point format. JavaScript makes no distinction between integers and floating-point numbers. Numeric literals appear in JavaScript programs using the usual syntax: a sequence of digits, with an optional decimal point and an optional exponent. For example:

```
1
3.14
.0001
6.02e23
```

Integers may also appear in octal or hexadecimal notation. An octal literal begins with 0, and a hexadecimal literal begins with 0x:

```
0377 // The number 255 in octal
0xFF // The number 255 in hexadecimal
```

When a numeric operation overflows, it returns a special value that represents positive or negative infinity. When an operation underflows, it returns zero. When an operation such as taking the square root of a negative number yields an error or meaningless result, it returns the special value NaN, which represents a value that is not-a-number. Use the global function isNaN() to test for this value.

The Number object defines useful numeric constants. The Math object defines various mathematical operations.

Booleans

The boolean type has two possible values, represented by the JavaScript keywords `true` and `false`. These values represent truth or falsehood, on or off, yes or no, or anything else that can be represented with one bit of information.

Strings

A JavaScript string is a sequence of arbitrary letters, digits, and other characters. The ECMA-262 standard requires JavaScript to support the full 16-bit Unicode character set. IE 4 supports Unicode, but Navigator 4 supports only the Latin-1 character set.

String literals appear in JavaScript programs between single or double quotes. One style of quotes may be nested within the other:

```
'testing'
"3.14"
'name="myform"'
"Wouldn't you prefer O'Reilly's book?"
```

When the backslash character (\) appears within a string literal, it changes or "escapes" the meaning of the character that follows it. The following table lists these special escape sequences:

Escape	Represents
\b	Backspace
\f	Form feed
\n	Newline
\r	Carriage return
\t	Tab
\'	Apostrophe or single quote that does not terminate the string

Escape	Represents
\"	Double-quote that does not terminate the string
\\	Single backslash character
\ddd	Character with Latin-1 encoding specified by three octal digits ddd
\xdd	Character with Latin-1 encoding specified by two hexadecimal digits dd
\udddd	Character with Unicode encoding specified by four hexadecimal digits dddd
\n	n, where n is any character other than those shown above

The String class defines many methods that you can use to operate on strings. It also defines the length property, which specifies the number of characters in a string.

The addition (+) operator concatenates strings. The equality (==) operator compares two strings to see if they contain exactly the same sequences of characters. (This is compare-by-value, not compare-by-reference, as C, C++, or Java programmers might expect.) The inequality operator (!=) does the reverse. The relational operators (<, <=, >, and >=) compare strings using alphabetical order.

JavaScript strings are *immutable,* which means that there is no way to change the contents of a string. Methods that operate on strings typically return a modified copy of the string.

Objects

An *object* is a compound data type that contains any number of properties. Each property has a name and a value. The . operator is used to access a named property of an object. For example, you can read and write property values of an object o as follows:

```
o.x = 1;
o.y = 2;
o.total = o.x + o.y;
```

Object properties are not defined in advance as they are in C, C++, or Java; any object can be assigned any property. JavaScript objects are associative arrays: they associate arbitrary data values with arbitrary names. Because of this fact, object properties can also be accessed using array notation:

```
o["x"] = 1;
o["y"] = 2;
```

Objects are created with the new operator. You can create a new object with no properties as follows:

```
var o = new Object();
```

Typically, however, you use predefined *constructors* to create objects that are members of a *class* of objects and have suitable properties and methods automatically defined. For example, you can create a Date object that represents the current time with:

```
var now = new Date();
```

You can also define your own object classes and corresponding constructors.

In JavaScript 1.2, you can use object literal syntax to include objects literally in a program. An object literal is a comma-separated list of name/value pairs, contained within curly braces. For example:

```
var o = {x:1, y:2, total:3};
```

Arrays

An array is a type of object that contains numbered values rather than named values. The [ ] operator is used to access the numbered values of an array:

```
a[0] = 1;
a[1] = a[0] + a[0];
```

The first element of a JavaScript array is element 0. Every array has a length property that specifies the number of elements in the array. The last element of an array is element length-1.

You create an array with the Array() constructor:

```
var a = new Array();        // Empty array
var b = new Array(10);      // 10 elements
var c = new Array(1,2,3);   // Elements 1,2,3
```

In JavaScript 1.2, you can use array literal syntax to include arrays directly in a program. An array literal is a comma-separated list of values enclosed within square brackets. For example:

```
var a = [1,2,3];
var b = [1, true, [1,2], {x:1, y:2}, "Hello"];
```

The Array class defines a number of useful methods for working with arrays.

Functions and methods

A function is a piece of JavaScript code that is defined once and can be executed multiple times by a program. A function definition looks like this:

```
function sum(x, y) {
    return x + y;
}
```

Functions are invoked using the () operator and passing a list of argument values:

```
var total = sum(1,2);    // Total is now 3
```

In JavaScript 1.1, you can create functions using the Function() constructor:

```
var sum = new Function("x", "y", "return x+y;");
```

In JavaScript 1.2, you can define functions using function literal syntax:

```
var sum = function(x,y) { return x+y; }
```

When a function is assigned to a property of an object, it is called a *method* of that object. Within the body of the function, the keyword `this` refers to the object for which the function is a property.

Within the body of a function, the `arguments[]` array contains the complete set of arguments passed to the function. The Function and Arguments classes represent functions and their arguments.

`null` *and undefined*

The JavaScript keyword `null` is a special value that indicates "no value". If a variable contains `null`, you know that it does not contain a valid value of any type. There is one other special value in JavaScript: the undefined value. This is the value returned when you use an undeclared or uninitialized variable or when you use a non-existent object property. There is no JavaScript keyword for this value.

Expressions and Operators

JavaScript expressions are formed by combining literal values and variables with JavaScript operators. Parentheses can be used in an expression to group subexpressions and alter the default order of evaluation of the expression. For example:

```
1+2
total/n
sum(o.x, a[3])++
(1+2)*3
```

JavaScript defines a complete set of operators, most of which should be familiar to all C, C++, and Java programmers. In the following table, the P column specifies operator precedence and the A column specifies operator associativity: L means left-to-right associativity, and R means right-to-left associativity.

P	A	Operator	Operation Performed
15	L	.	Access an object property
	L	[]	Access an array element
	L	( )	Invoke a function
14	R	++	Unary pre- or post-increment
	R	- -	Unary pre- or post-decrement
	R	-	Unary minus (negation)
	R	~	Numeric bitwise complement
	R	!	Unary boolean complement
	R	delete	Undefine a property (1.2)
	R	new	Create a new object
	R	typeof	Return type of operand (1.1)
	R	void	Return undefined value (1.1)
13	L	*, /, %	Multiplication, division, modulo
12	L	+,-	Addition, subtraction
	L	+	String concatenation
11	L	<<	Integer shift left
	L	>>	Shift right, sign extension
	L	>>>	Shift right, zero extension
10	L	<, <=	Less than, less than or equal
	L	>, >=	Greater than, greater than or equal
9	L	==, !=	Test for equality or inequality
	L	===, !==	Test for identity or non-identity (no type conversion)
8	L	&	Integer bitwise AND
7	L	^	Integer bitwise XOR
6	L			Integer bitwise OR
5	L	&&	Logical AND; evaluate 2nd operand only if 1st is true
4	L	||	Logical OR; evaluate 2nd operand only if 1st is false
3	R	?:	Conditional: *if?then:else*

P	A	Operator	Operation Performed
2	R	=	Assignment
	R	*=, +=, -=, etc.	Assignment with operation
1	L	,	Multiple evaluation

Statements

A JavaScript program is a sequence of JavaScript statements. Most JavaScript statements have the same syntax as the corresponding C, C++, and Java statements:

Expression statements

Every JavaScript expression can stand alone as a statement. Assignments, method calls, increments, and decrements are expression statements. For example:

```
s = "hello world";
x = Math.sqrt(4);
x++
```

Compound statements

When a sequence of JavaScript statements is enclosed within curly braces, it counts as a single compound statement. For example, the body of a `while` loop consists of a single statement. If you want the loop to execute more than one statement, use a compound statement. This is a common technique with `if`, `for`, and other statements described later.

Empty statements

The empty statement is simply a semicolon by itself. It does nothing, and is occasionally useful for coding empty loop bodies.

Labeled statements

In JavaScript 1.2, any statement can be labeled with a name. Labeled loops can then be used with the labeled versions of the `break` and `continue` statements:

```
label : statement
```

break

> The break statement terminates execution of the inner-most enclosing loop, or, in JavaScript 1.2, the named loop:
>
> ```
> break ;
> break label ;     // JavaScript 1.2
> ```

case

> case is not a true statement. Instead it is a keyword used to label statements within a JavaScript 1.2 switch statement:
>
> ```
> case constant-expression :
>     statements
>     [ break ; ]
> ```
>
> Because of the nature of the switch statement, a group of statements labeled by case should usually end with a break statement.

continue

> The continue statement restarts the innermost enclosing loop, or, in JavaScript 1.2, restarts the named loop:
>
> ```
> continue ;
> continue label ;    //JavaScript 1.2
> ```

default

> Like case, default is not a true statement, but instead a label that may appear within a JavaScript 1.2 switch statement:
>
> ```
> default:
>     statements
>     [ break ; ]
> ```

do/while

> The do/while loop repeatedly executes a statement while an expression is true. It is like the while loop, except that the loop condition appears (and is tested) at the bottom of the loop. This means that the body of the loop will be executed at least once:

```
do
    statement
while ( expression ) ;
```

This statement is new in JavaScript 1.2. In Navigator 4, the
continue statement does not work correctly within do/
while loops.

export
    The export statement was introduced in Navigator 4. It
    makes the specified functions and properties accessible to
    other windows or execution contexts:

```
export expression [, expression... ];
```

for
    The for statement is an easy-to-use loop that combines
    the initialization and increment expressions with the loop
    condition expression:

```
for (initialize ; test ; increment)
    statement
```

The for loop repeatedly executes a statement as long as
its test expression is true. It evaluates the initialization
expression once before starting the loop and evaluates
the increment expression at the end of each iteration.

for/in
    The for/in statement loops through the properties of a
    specified object:

```
for (variable in object)
    statement
```

The for/in loop executes a statement once for each
property of an object. Each time through the loop, it
assigns the name of the current property to the specified
variable. Some properties of pre-defined JavaScript
objects are not enumerated by the for/in loop. User-
defined properties are always enumerated.

function
    The function statement defines a function in a JavaScript
    program:

```
function funcname(args) {
    statements
}
```

This statement defines a function named *funcname*, with a body that consists of the specified statement, and arguments as specified by *args*. *args* is a comma-separated list of zero or more argument names. These arguments can be used in the body of the function to refer to the parameter values passed to the function.

if/else

The if statement executes a statement if an expression is true:

```
if ( expression )
    statement
```

When an else clause is added, the statement executes a different statement if the expression is false:

```
if ( expression )
    statement
else
    statement2
```

Any else clause may be combined with a nested if/else statement to produce an else if statement:

```
if ( expression )
    statement
else if ( expression2 )
    statement2
else
    statement3
```

import

The import statement was introduced in Navigator 4 along with export. It makes the named functions and variables available in the current window or execution context, or, in the second form of the statement, makes all properties and methods of the specified object available within the current context:

```
import expression [, expression];
import expression.* ;
```

return

The return statement causes the currently executing
function to stop executing and return to its caller. If followed by an expression, the value of that expression is
used as the function return value.

```
return ;
return expression ;
```

switch

The switch statement is a multi-way branch. It evaluates
an expression and then jumps to a statement that is
labeled with a case clause that matches the value of the
expression. If no matching case label is found, the
switch statement jumps to the statement, if any, labeled
with default:

```
switch ( expression ) {
    case constant-expression: statements
    [ case constant-expression: statements ]
    [ ... ]
    default: statements
}
```

var

The var statement declares and optionally initializes one
or more variables. Variable declaration is optional in top-
level code, but is required to declare local variables within
function bodies:

```
var name [ = value ] [ , name2 [ = value2 ] ... ] ;
```

while

The while statement is a basic loop. It repeatedly executes a statement while an expression is true:

```
while ( expression )
    statement ;
```

with

The with statement adds an object to the scope chain, so
that a statement is interpreted in the context of the object:

```
with ( object )
    statement ;
```

The use of with statements is discouraged.

Regular Expressions

JavaScript 1.2 supports regular expressions, using the same syntax as Perl 4. A regular expression is specified literally as a sequence of characters within forward slashes (/), or as a JavaScript string passed to the RegExp() constructor. The optional g (global search) and i (case-insensitive search) modifiers may follow the second / character, or may be passed to RegExp().

The following table summarizes regular expression syntax:

Character	Meaning
\n, \r, \t	Match literal newline, carriage return, tab
\\, \/, *, \+, \?, etc.	Match a special character literally, ignoring or escaping its special meaning
[...]	Match any one character between brackets
[^...]	Match any one character not between brackets
.	Match any character other than newline
\w, \W	Match any word/non-word character
\s, \S	Match any whitespace/non-whitespace
\d, \D	Match any digit/non-digit
^, $	Require match at beginning/end of a string, or in multi-line mode, beginning/end of a line
\b, \B	Require match at a word boundary non-boundary
?	Optional term; Match zero or one time
+	Match previous term one or more times
*	Match term zero or more times

Character	Meaning
{*n*}	Match previous term exactly *n* times
{*n*,}	Match previous term *n* or more times
{*n*,*m*}	Match at least *n* but no more than *m* times
a | *b*	Match either *a* or *b*
(*sub*)	Group sub-expression *sub* into a single term, and remember the text that it matched
n	Match exactly the same characters that were matched by sub-expression number *n*
$*n*	In replacement strings, substitute the text that matched the *n*th sub-expression

JavaScript in HTML

Client-side JavaScript code may be embedded in HTML files in several ways:

<SCRIPT> tag

Most JavaScript code appears in HTML files between a <SCRIPT> tag and a </SCRIPT> tag. The <SCRIPT> tag can also be used to include an external file of JavaScript code into an HTML document. The <SCRIPT> tag supports a number of attributes, including these three important ones:

LANGUAGE

Specifies the scripting language in which the script is written. In most browsers, this attribute defaults to "JavaScript". You must set it if you are mixing scripting languages, such as JavaScript and VBScript.

Set this attribute to "JavaScript1.1" to specify that the code uses JavaScript 1.1 features, and that it should not be interpreted by JavaScript 1.0 browsers. Set this attribute to "JavaScript1.2" to specify that only Java Script 1.2 browsers should interpret the code. (Note,

---

however, that Navigator 4 has some non-standard
behaviors when "JavaScript1.2" is specified.)

SRC

Specifies the URL of an external script to be loaded
and executed. Files of JavaScript code typically have a
.js extension. Note that the `</SCRIPT>` tag is still
required when this attribute is used. Supported in JavaScript 1.1 and later.

ARCHIVE

Specifies the URL of a JAR file that contains the script
specified by the SRC attribute. Supported in JavaScript
1.2 and later. Archives are required to use Navigator 4
signed scripts.

Event handlers

JavaScript code may also appear as the value of event
handler attributes of HTML tags. Event handler attributes
always begin with "on". The code specified by one of
these attributes is executed when the named event
occurs. For example, the following HTML specifies a button that displays a dialog box when clicked:

```
<INPUT TYPE=button VALUE="Press Me"
       onClick="alert('hello world!');">
```

JavaScript URLs

JavaScript code may appear in a URL that uses the special
javascript: pseudo-protocol. The JavaScript code is
evaluated, and the resulting value (converted to a string,
if necessary) is used as the contents of the URL. Use the
void operator if you want a JavaScript URL that executes
JavaScript statements without overwriting the current
document:

```
<FORM ACTION="javascript:void validate()">
```

JavaScript entities

In JavaScript 1.1, HTML attribute values may contain JavaScript code in the form of JavaScript entities. An HTML
entity is a string like `&lt;` that represents some other char-

---

acter or string. A JavaScript entity is JavaScript code contained within &{ and };. Its value is the value of the JavaScript expression within:

```
<BODY BGCOLOR="&{getFavoriteColor()};">
```

Client-Side Object Hierarchy

Client-side JavaScript has access to a suite of client-side objects that represent the browser, browser windows and frames, HTML documents, and elements within HTML documents. These objects are structured in a hierarchy as shown in Figure 1.

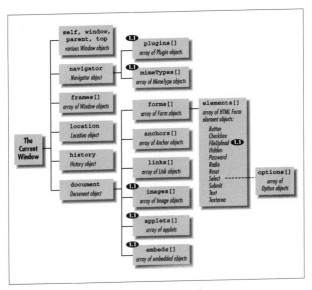

Figure 1. The client-side object hierarchy

Windows and Frames

The Window object represents a browser window or frame in client-side JavaScript. Each Window object has properties that refer to its nested frames, if any, and its containing window or frame, if any. Figure 2 illustrates these properties.

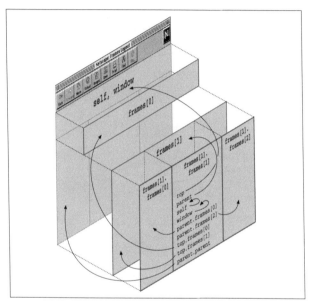

Figure 2. Windows and frames

Forms

One of the powerful features of JavaScript is its ability to manipulate HTML forms. HTML defines the following form elements:

Button (<INPUT TYPE=button>)
    A graphical push button; onClick events

Checkbox (<INPUT TYPE=checkbox>)
    A toggle button without mutually-exclusive behavior; onClick events

FileUpload (<INPUT TYPE=file>)
    A file entry field and file browser; onChange events

Hidden (<INPUT TYPE=hidden>)
    A non-visual data field; no event handlers

Option (<OPTION>)
    An item within a Select list; event handlers are on the Select object, not Option objects

Password (<INPUT TYPE=password>)
    An input field for sensitive data; onChange events

Radio (<INPUT TYPE=radio>)
    A toggle button with mutually-exclusive "radio" behavior; onClick events

Reset (<INPUT TYPE=reset>)
    A button that resets a form; onClick events

Select (<SELECT[MULTIPLE]>...</SELECT>)
    A list or drop-down menu from which one or more Option items may be selected; onChange events

Submit (<INPUT TYPE=submit>)
    A button that submits a form; onClick events

Text (<INPUT TYPE=text>)
    A single-line text entry field; onChange events

TextArea (<TEXTAREA>...</TEXTAREA>)
    A multi-line text entry fields; onChange events

Figure 3 shows a web page that contains each type of form element.

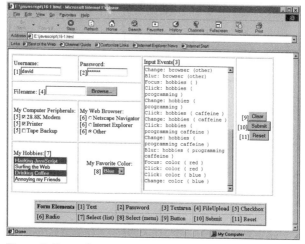

Figure 3. Form elements

Events

Client-side JavaScript supports a number of event types. The following table lists the event handlers and the client-side objects that support the handlers. Note that some events, such as `onDblClick`, are not reliably generated on all platforms.

Event Handler	Supported By
onAbort	Image (JavaScript 1.1)
onBlur, onFocus	Text elements; Window and all other form elements (1.1)
onChange	Select, text input elements
onClick	Button elements, Link. Return `false` to cancel default action.
onDblClick	Document, Link, Image, Button elements (1.2)
onError	Image, Window (1.1)

Event Handler	Supported By
`onKeyDown,` `onKeyPress,` `onKeyUp`	Document, Image, Link, text elements (1.2). Return `false` to cancel.
`onLoad,` `onUnload`	Window; Image in 1.1
`onMouseDown,` `onMouseUp`	Document, Link, Image, Button elements (1.2). Return `false` to cancel.
`onMouseOver,` `onMouseOut`	Link; Image and Layer (1.2). Return `true` to prevent URL display.
`onReset,` `onSubmit`	Form (1.1). Return `false` to prevent reset or submission.

JavaScript Security Restrictions

For security reasons, there are restrictions on the tasks that untrusted JavaScript code can perform. In Navigator 4, signed scripts can circumvent these restrictions by requesting certain privileges:

Same origin policy
> Scripts can only read properties of windows and documents that were loaded from the same web server unless they have `UniversalBrowserRead`.

User's browsing history
> Scripts cannot read the array of URLs from the History object without `UniversalBrowserRead`.

File uploads
> Scripts cannot set the value property of the FileUpload form element without `UniversalBrowserRead`.

Sending email and posting news
> Scripts cannot submit forms to a `mailto:` or `news:` URL without user confirmation or `UniversalSendMail`.

Closing windows

A script can only close browser windows that it created, unless it gets user confirmation or has `UniversalBrowserWrite`.

Snooping in the cache

A script cannot load any `about:` URLs, such as `about:cache`, without `UniversalBrowserRead`.

Hidden windows and window decorations

A script cannot create small or offscreen windows or windows without a titlebar, and cannot show or hide window decorations without `UniversalBrowserWrite`.

Intercepting or spoofing events

A script cannot capture events from windows or documents from a different server and cannot set the fields of an Event object without `UniversalBrowserWrite`.

Reading and setting preferences

A script cannot read or write user preferences using `Navigator.preference()` without `UniversalPreferencesRead` or `UniversalPreferencesWrite`.

Global Properties

Core JavaScript defines two global constants:

`Infinity`

A numeric constant that represents infinity. Internet Explorer 4; ECMA-262; not supported by Navigator 4.

`NaN`

The not-a-number constant. Internet Explorer 4; ECMA-262; not supported by Navigator 4.

In addition to these core global properties, the Window object defines a number of client-side global properties.

Global Functions

Core JavaScript defines a handful of global functions:

`escape(s)`
> Encode a string for transmission. JavaScript 1.0; ECMA-262; Unicode support in Internet Explorer 4.

`eval(code)`
> Execute JavaScript code from a string.

`getClass(javaobj)`
> Return the JavaClass of a JavaObject. Navigator 3.

`isFinite(n)`
> Determine whether a number is finite. JavaScript 1.2; ECMA-262.

`isNaN(x)`
> Check for not-a-number. JavaScript 1.1; ECMA-262.

`parseFloat(s)`
> Convert a string to a number. JavaScript 1.0; enhanced in JavaScript 1.1; ECMA-262.

`parseInt(s, radix)`
> Convert a string to an integer. JavaScript 1.0; enhanced in JavaScript 1.1; ECMA-262.

`unescape(s)`
> Decode an escaped string. JavaScript 1.0; ECMA-262; Unicode support in Internet Explorer 4.

In addition to these core global functions, the Window object defines a number of client-side global methods.

Alphabetical Object Reference

Anchor   the target of a hypertext link

Availability

Client-side JavaScript 1.2

Inherits From

HTMLElement

Synopsis

```
document.anchors[i]
document.anchors.length
```

Properties

Anchor inherits properties from HTMLElement and also
defines or overrides the following:

name
> The name of an anchor.

text
> The text of an anchor. Navigator 4.

x
> The X-coordinate of an anchor. Navigator 4.

y
> The Y-coordinate of an anchor. Navigator 4.

Applet   an applet embedded in a web page

Availability

Client-side JavaScript 1.1

Synopsis

```
document.applets[i]
document.appletName
```

Properties

The properties of an Applet object are the same as the public fields of the Java applet it represents.

Methods

The methods of an Applet object are the same as the public methods of the Java applet it represents.

Area   see Link

Arguments

arguments and other properties of a function

Availability

Core JavaScript 1.1; ECMA-262; only defined within a function body

Synopsis

```
arguments
```

Properties

callee
> The function that is currently running. JavaScript 1.2; ECMA-262.

caller
> The calling context. Navigator 4.

length
> The number of arguments passed to a function.

Array built-in support for arrays

Availability

Core JavaScript 1.1; enhanced by ECMA-262; enhanced in
Navigator 4. Array functionality is available in JavaScript 1.0,
but the Array object itself is not supported by Navigator 2.

Constructor

```
new Array()
new Array(size)
new Array(element0, element1,..., elementn)
```

Properties

length
> The size of an array. JavaScript 1.1, Internet Explorer 3;
> ECMA-262.

Methods

concat(value,...)
> Concatenate arrays. JavaScript 1.2.

join(separator)
> Concatenate array elements to form a string. JavaScript
> 1.1; ECMA-262.

pop()
> Remove and return the last element of an array. Navigator
> 4.

push(value,...)
> Append elements to an array. Navigator 4.

reverse()
> Reverse the elements of an array. JavaScript 1.1; ECMA-
> 262.

shift()
> Shift array elements down. Navigator 4.

slice(*start, end*)
Return a portion of an array. JavaScript 1.2.

sort(*orderfunc*)
Sort the elements of an array. JavaScript 1.1; ECMA-262.

splice(*start, deleteCount, value,...*)
Insert, remove, or replace array elements. Navigator 4.

toString()
Convert an array to a string. JavaScript 1.1; ECMA-262.

unshift(*value,...*)
Insert elements at the beginning of an array. Navigator 4.

Boolean   support for boolean values

Availability

Core JavaScript 1.1; ECMA-262

Constructor

```
// Constructor function
new Boolean(value)
// Conversion function
Boolean(value)
```

Methods

toString()
Convert a boolean value to a string.

Button   a graphical pushbutton

Availability

Client-side JavaScript 1.0; enhanced in JavaScript 1.1

Inherits From

Input, HTMLElement

Synopsis

```
form.name
form.elements[i]
```

Properties

Button inherits properties from Input and HTMLElement and also defines or overrides the following:

`value`
  The text that appears in a Button.

Methods

Button inherits methods from Input and HTMLElement.

Event Handlers

Button inherits event handlers from Input and HTMLElement and also defines or overrides the following:

`onclick`
  The handler invoked when a Button is clicked.

Checkbox   a graphical checkbox

Availability

Client-side JavaScript 1.0; enhanced in JavaScript 1.1

Inherits From

Input, HTMLElement

Synopsis

```
// A single checkbox with a unique name
form.name
form.elements[i]
// A group of checkboxes with the same name
form.name[i]
```

Properties

Checkbox inherits properties from Input and HTMLElement and also defines or overrides the following:

checked
> Whether a Checkbox is checked.

defaultChecked
> The initial state of a Checkbox.

value
> The value returned when a form is submitted.

Methods

Checkbox inherits the methods of Input and HTMLElement.

Event Handlers

Checkbox inherits event handlers from Input and HTMLElement and also defines or overrides the following:

onclick
> The handler invoked when a Checkbox is selected.

Crypto   cryptography-related resources

Availability

Client-side Navigator 4.04 and later

Synopsis

    crypto

Functions

crypto.random(*numbytes*)
> Generate random byte strings.

crypto.signText(*text, CASelection, allowedCA...*)
> Ask the user to digitally sign text.

Date   manipulate dates and times

Availability

Core JavaScript 1.0; enhanced by ECMA-262

Constructor

```
new Date();
new Date(milliseconds)
new Date(datestring);
new Date(year, month, day, hours, minutes,
         seconds, ms)
```

Methods

Note that unlike most JavaScript objects, the Date object has no properties that can be read and written directly; instead, all access to date and time fields is done through methods:

getDate()
> Return the day of the month. JavaScript 1.0; ECMA-262.

getDay()
> Return the day of the week. JavaScript 1.0; ECMA-262.

getFullYear()
> Return the year (local time). JavaScript 1.2; ECMA-262.

getHours()
> Return the hours field of a Date. JavaScript 1.0; ECMA-262.

getMilliseconds()
> Return the milliseconds field of a Date (local time).
> JavaScript 1.2; ECMA-262.

getMinutes()
> Return the minutes field of a Date. JavaScript 1.0; ECMA-262.

getMonth()
> Return the month of a Date. JavaScript 1.0; ECMA-262.

`getSeconds()`
> Return the seconds field of a Date. JavaScript 1.0;
> ECMA-262.

`getTime()`
> Return a Date in milliseconds. JavaScript 1.0; ECMA-262.

`getTimezoneOffset()`
> Determine the offset from GMT. JavaScript 1.0; ECMA-262.

`getUTCDate()`
> Return the day of the month (universal time). JavaScript
> 1.2; ECMA-262.

`getUTCDay()`
> Return the day of the week (universal time). JavaScript
> 1.2; ECMA-262.

`getUTCFullYear()`
> Return the year (universal time). JavaScript 1.2; ECMA-
> 262.

`getUTCHours()`
> Return the hours field of a Date (universal time).
> JavaScript 1.2; ECMA-262.

`getUTCMilliseconds()`
> Return the milliseconds field of a Date (universal time).
> JavaScript 1.2; ECMA-262.

`getUTCMinutes()`
> Return the minutes field of a Date (universal time).
> JavaScript 1.2; ECMA-262.

`getUTCMonth()`
> Return the month of the year (universal time). JavaScript
> 1.2; ECMA-262.

`getUTCSeconds()`
> Return the seconds field of a Date (universal time).
> JavaScript 1.2; ECMA-262.

getYear()

> Return the year field of a Date. JavaScript 1.0; ECMA-262; deprecated in JavaScript 1.2 in favor of getFullYear ().

setDate(*day_of_month*)

> Set the day of the month. JavaScript 1.0; ECMA-262.

setFullYear(*year*)

> Set the year (local time). JavaScript 1.2; ECMA-262.

setHours(*hours*)

> Set the hours field of a Date. JavaScript 1.0; ECMA-262.

setMilliseconds(*millis*)

> Set the milliseconds field of a Date (local time). JavaScript 1.2; ECMA-262.

setMinutes(*minutes*)

> Set the minutes field of a Date. JavaScript 1.0; ECMA-262.

setMonth(*month*)

> Set the month field of a Date. JavaScript 1.0; ECMA-262.

setSeconds(*seconds*)

> Set the seconds field of a Date. JavaScript 1.0; ECMA-262.

setTime(*milliseconds*)

> Set a Date in milliseconds. JavaScript 1.0; ECMA-262.

setUTCDate(*day_of_month*)

> Set the day of the month (universal time). JavaScript 1.2; ECMA-262.

setUTCFullYear(*year*)

> Set the year (universal time). JavaScript 1.2; ECMA-262.

setUTCHours(*hours*)

> Set the hours field of a Date (universal time). JavaScript 1.2; ECMA-262.

setUTCMilliseconds(*millis*)

> Set the milliseconds field of a Date (universal time). JavaScript 1.2; ECMA-262.

setUTCMinutes(*minutes*)

> Set the minutes field of a Date (universal time). JavaScript 1.2; ECMA-262.

`setUTCMonth(`*`month`*`)`
> Set the month (universal time). JavaScript 1.2; ECMA-262.

`setUTCSeconds(`*`seconds`*`)`
> Set the seconds field of a Date (universal time). JavaScript 1.2; ECMA-262.

`setYear(`*`year`*`)`
> Set the year field of a Date. JavaScript 1.0; ECMA-262; deprecated in JavaScript 1.2 in favor of `setFullYear()`.

`toGMTString()`
> Convert a date to a universal time string. JavaScript 1.0; ECMA-262; deprecated in JavaScript 1.2 in favor of `toUTCString()`.

`toLocaleString()`
> Convert a Date to a string. JavaScript 1.0; ECMA-262.

`toString()`
> Convert a date to a string. JavaScript 1.0; ECMA-262.

`toUTCString()`
> Convert a date to a string (universal time). JavaScript 1.2; ECMA-262.

`valueOf()`
> Convert a date to a number. JavaScript 1.1; ECMA-262.

Static Methods

`Date.parse(`*`date`*`)`
> Parse a date/time string. JavaScript 1.0; ECMA-262.

`Date.UTC(`*`year, month, day, hours, minutes, seconds, ms`*`)`
> Convert a date specification to milliseconds. JavaScript 1.0; ECMA-262.

Document

represents an HTML document

Availability

Client-side JavaScript 1.0; enhanced in JavaScript 1.1 and in Navigator 4 and Internet Explorer 4

Inherits From

HTMLElement

Synopsis

```
window.document
document
```

Properties

Document inherits properties from HTMLElement and also defines numerous properties. Navigator 4 and Internet Explorer 4 both define a number of incompatible Document properties, used mostly for DHTML; they are listed separately after the generic properties:

alinkColor
    The color of activated links.

anchors[]
    The Anchors in a document. JavaScript 1.0; array elements are null prior to JavaScript 1.2.

applets[]
    The applets in a document. JavaScript 1.1.

bgColor
    The document background color.

cookie
    The cookie(s) of the document.

domain
    The security domain of a document. JavaScript 1.1.

embeds[]
    The objects embedded in a document. JavaScript 1.1.

fgColor
> The default text color.

forms[]
> The Forms in a document.

images[]
> The images embedded in a document. JavaScript 1.1.

lastModified
> The modification date of a document.

linkColor
> The color of unfollowed links.

links[]
> The Link objects in a document.

location
> The URL of the current document. JavaScript 1.0; deprecated in JavaScript 1.1 in favor of Document.URL.

plugins[]
> The objects embedded in a document. JavaScript 1.1.

referrer
> The URL of the linked-from document. JavaScript 1.0; non-functional in Internet Explorer 3.

title
> The title of a document.

URL
> The URL of the current document. JavaScript 1.1.

vlinkColor
> The color of visited links.

Navigator 4 Properties

classes
> Define style classes.

height
> The height of a document.

ids
> Define styles for individual tags.

layers[]
> The layers contained in a document.

tags
> Define styles for HTML tags.

width
> The width of a document.

Internet Explorer 4 Properties

activeElement
> Which input element has the focus.

all[]
> All HTML elements in a document.

charset
> The character set in use.

children[]
> The child elements of the document.

defaultCharset
> The default character set of a document.

expando
> Disallow new property creation.

parentWindow
> The window of a document.

readyState
> The loading status of a document.

Methods

Document inherits methods from HTMLElement and also defines some methods. Navigator 4 and IE 4 both define a number of incompatible Document methods, used mostly for DHTML; they are listed separately after the generic methods:

clear()
> Clear a document. JavaScript 1.0; deprecated.

---

close()
   Close an output stream.

open(*mimetype*)
   Begin a new document.

write(*value,...*)
   Append data to a document.

writeln(*value,...*)
   Append data and a newline to a document.

Navigator 4 Methods

captureEvents(*eventmask*)
   Specify event types to be captured.

contextual(*style1, style2,...*)
   Define a contextual style.

getSelection()
   Return the selected text.

releaseEvents(*eventmask*)
   Stop capturing events.

routeEvent(*event*)
   Pass a captured event to the next handler.

Internet Explorer 4 Methods

elementFromPoint(*x, y*)
   Determine which HTML element is at a given point.

Event Handlers

The <BODY> tag has onLoad and onUnload attributes. Technically, however, the onload and onunload event handlers belong to the Window object, rather than the Document object.

Event

details about an event

Availability

Client-side JavaScript; incompatible versions are supported by Navigator 4 and Internet Explorer 4

Synopsis

```
// Event handler argument in Navigator 4
function handler (event) {...}
// Window property in IE 4
window.event
```

Navigator 4 Properties

data

    Data from a DragDrop event. Requires Universal-BrowserWrite privilege to set; requires Universal-BrowserRead privilege to read.

height

    The new height of a resized window or frame.

layerX

    The X-coordinate, within a layer, of the event.

layerY

    The Y-coordinate, within a layer, of the event.

modifiers

    Which modifiers keys are held down.

pageX

    The X-coordinate, within a page, of the event.

pageY

    The Y-coordinate, within a page, of the event.

screenX

    The screen X-coordinate of the event. JavaScript 1.2.

screenY

    The screen Y-coordinate of the event. JavaScript 1.2.

`target`
> The object on which the event occurred.

`type`
> The type of the event. JavaScript 1.2.

TYPE
> Static event type constants for bitmasks.

`which`
> Which key or mouse button was clicked.

`width`
> The new width of a resized window or frame.

`x`
> The X-coordinate of the event within a positioned element. JavaScript 1.2.

`y`
> The Y-coordinate of the event within a positioned element. JavaScript 1.2.

Internet Explorer 4 Properties

`altKey`
> Whether the **ALT** key was pressed during an event.

`button`
> Which mouse button was pressed.

`cancelBubble`
> Stop event propagation.

`clientX`
> The X-coordinate, within a page, of the event.

`clientY`
> The Y-coordinate, within a page, of the event.

`ctrlKey`
> Whether the **CTRL** key was pressed during an event.

`fromElement`
> The object the mouse is moving from.

`keyCode`
> The Unicode encoding of the key typed.

---

offsetX
: The X-coordinate of the event, relative to the container.

offsetY
: The Y-coordinate of the event, relative to the container.

reason
: Data transfer status.

returnValue
: Specify a return value for the event handler.

screenX
: The screen X-coordinate of the event. JavaScript 1.2.

screenY
: The screen Y-coordinate of the event. JavaScript 1.2.

shiftKey
: Whether the **SHIFT** key was pressed during an event.

srcElement
: The object on which the event occurred.

srcFilter
: The filter that changed.

toElement
: The object to which the mouse is moving.

type
: The type of the event. JavaScript 1.2.

x
: The X-coordinate of the event within a positioned element. JavaScript 1.2.

y
: The Y-coordinate of the event within a positioned element. JavaScript 1.2.

FileUpload

a file upload field for form input

Availability

Client-side JavaScript 1.0

Inherits From

Input, HTMLElement

Synopsis

form.name
form.elements[*i*]

Properties

FileUpload inherits properties from Input and HTMLElement
and defines or overrides the following:

value
  The filename selected by the user. JavaScript 1.1.

Methods

FileUpload inherits methods from Input and HTMLElement.

Event Handlers

FileUpload inherits event handlers from Input and HTMLElement and defines or overrides the following:

onchange
  The handler invoked when input value changes.

Form   an HTML input form

Availability

Client-side JavaScript 1.0

Inherits From

HTMLElement

Synopsis

document.form_name
document.forms[*form_number*]

Properties

Form inherits properties from HTMLElement and also defines or overrides the following:

action
>   The URL for form submission. JavaScript 1.0; read-only in Internet Explorer 3.

elements[]
>   The input elements of the form.

elements.length
>   The number of elements in a form.

encoding
>   The encoding of form data. JavaScript 1.0; read-only in Internet Explorer 3.

length
>   The number of elements in a form.

method
>   The submission method for the form. JavaScript 1.0; read-only in Internet Explorer 3.

name
>   The name of a form.

target
>   The window for form results. JavaScript 1.0; read-only in Internet Explorer 3.

Methods

Form inherits methods from HTMLElement and also defines the following:

reset()
>   Reset the elements of a form. JavaScript 1.1.

submit()
>   Submit a form.

Event Handlers

Form inherits event handlers from HTMLElement and also defines the following:

onreset
>   The handler invoked when a form is reset. JavaScript 1.1.

onsubmit
>   Invoked when a form is submitted.

Frame   a type of Window object; see Window

Availability

Client-side JavaScript 1.0

Synopsis

```
window.frames[i]
window.frames.length
frames[i]
frames.length
```

Function   a JavaScript function

Availability

Core JavaScript 1.0; enhanced in JavaScript 1.1 and 1.2

Synopsis

```
// Function definition statement
function functionname(argument_name_list)
{
    body
}
// Unnamed function literal; JavaScript 1.2
function (argument_name_list ) { body}
// Function invocation
functionname(argument _value_list)
```

Constructor

```
// JavaScript 1.1 and later
new Function(argument_names, body)
```

Properties

arguments[]
> Arguments passed to a function. JavaScript 1.0; ECMA-262; deprecated in favor of the Arguments object.

arity
> The number of declared arguments. Navigator 4, with LANGUAGE="JavaScript1.2".

caller
> The function that called this one.

length
> The number of declared arguments. JavaScript 1.1; ECMA-262.

prototype
> The prototype for a class of objects. JavaScript 1.1.

Methods

apply(thisobj, args)
> Invoke a function as a method of an object. Navigator 4.

toString()
> Convert a function to a string. JavaScript 1.0; ECMA-262.

Hidden   hidden data for client/server communication

Availability

Client-side JavaScript 1.0; enhanced in JavaScript 1.1

Inherits From

Input, HTMLElement

Synopsis

```
form.name
form.elements[i]
```

Properties

Hidden inherits properties from Input and HTMLElement and
defines or overrides the following:

value
    Arbitrary data submitted with a form.

History   the URL history of the browser

Availability

Client-side JavaScript 1.0; additional features available in
Navigator 4 with the UniversalBrowserRead privilege

Synopsis

```
window.history
frame.history
history
```

Properties

current
    The URL of the currently displayed document. Navigator
    4; requires UniversalBrowserRead.

length
    The number of elements in the history array. Navigator 2,
    Internet Explorer 4.

next
    The URL of the next document in the history array. Navi-
    gator 4; requires UniversalBrowserRead.

previous
    The URL of the previous document in the history array.
    Navigator 4; requires UniversalBrowserRead.

Methods

back()

Return to the previous URL. JavaScript 1.0.

forward()

Visit the next URL. JavaScript 1.0.

go(*relative_position, target_string*).

Revisit a URL. JavaScript 1.0; enhanced in JavaScript 1.1.

toString()

Return browsing history, formatted in HTML. Navigator 4; requires UniversalBrowserRead.

HTMLElement   the superclass of all HTML elements

Availability

Client-side JavaScript 1.2

Internet Explorer 4 Properties

all[]

All elements contained within an element.

children[]

The direct children of an element.

className

The value of the CLASS attribute.

document

The Document object that contains an element.

id

The value of the ID attribute.

innerHTML

The HTML text contained within the element.

innerText

The text within the element.

lang

The value of the LANG attribute.

---

offsetHeight
> The height of the element.

offsetLeft
> The X-coordinate of the element.

offsetParent
> Defines the coordinate system of the element.

offsetTop
> The Y-coordinate of the element.

offsetWidth
> The width of the element.

outerHTML
> The HTML of an element.

outerText
> The text of an element.

parentElement
> The container of an element.

sourceIndex
> The index of the element in Document.all[].

style
> The inline CSS style of the element.

tagName
> The tag type of an element.

title
> Tool tip for an element.

Navigator 4 Methods

handleEvent(*event*)
> Pass an event to an appropriate handler.

Internet Explorer 4 Methods

contains(*target*)
> Whether one element is contained in another.

getAttribute(*name*)
> Get an attribute value.

insertAdjacentHTML(*where, text*)
    Insert HTML text before or after an element.

insertAdjacentText(*where, text*)
    Insert plain text before or after an element.

removeAttribute(*name*)
    Delete an attribute.

scrollIntoView(*top*)
    Make an element visible.

setAttribute(*name, value*)
    Set the value of an attribute.

Event Handlers

onclick
    The handler invoked when the user clicks on an element.
    JavaScript 1.2; HTML 4.0.

ondblclick
    The handler invoked when the user double-clicks on an
    element. JavaScript 1.2; HTML 4.0.

onhelp
    The handler invoked when the user presses F1. Internet
    Explorer 4.

onkeydown
    The handler invoked when the user presses a key. Java-
    Script 1.2; HTML 4.0.

onkeypress
    The handler invoked when the user presses a key. Java-
    Script 1.2; HTML 4.0.

onkeyup
    The handler invoked when the user releases a key. Java-
    Script 1.2; HTML 4.0.

onmousedown
    The handler invoked when the user presses a mouse but-
    ton. JavaScript 1.2; HTML 4.0.

onmousemove
> The handler invoked when mouse moves within an element. JavaScript 1.2; HTML 4.0.

onmouseout
> The handler invoked when mouse moves out of an element. JavaScript 1.2; HTML 4.0.

onmouseover
> The handler invoked when mouse moves over an element. JavaScript 1.2; HTML 4.0.

onmouseup
> The handler invoked when the user releases a mouse button. JavaScript 1.2; HTML 4.0.

Image   an image embedded in an HTML document

Availability

Client-side JavaScript 1.1

Inherits From

HTMLElement

Synopsis

```
document.images[i]
document.images.length
document.image-name
```

Constructor

```
new Image(width, height)
```

Properties

Image inherits properties from HTMLElement and defines or overrides the following:

border
> The border width of an image.

---

complete
> Whether an image load is complete.

height
> The height of an image.

hspace
> The horizontal padding for an image.

lowsrc
> An alternate image for low-resolution displays.

name
> The name of an image.

src
> The URL of the embedded image.

vspace
> The vertical padding for an image.

width
> The width of an image.

Event Handlers

Image inherits event handlers from HTMLElement and also defines the following:

onabort
> The handler invoked when user aborts image loading.

onerror
> The handler invoked when an error occurs during image loading.

onload
> Handler invoked when an image finishes loading.

Input   an input element in an HTML form

Availability

Client-side JavaScript 1.0; enhanced in JavaScript 1.1

Inherits From

HTMLElement

Synopsis

```
form.elements[i]
form.name
```

Properties

Input inherits properties from HTMLElement and defines or
overrides the following:

checked
> Whether a Checkbox or Radio element is checked.

defaultChecked
> A Checkbox or Radio element's default status.

defaultValue
> The default text displayed in an element.

form
> The Form containing the element.

name
> The name of a form element.

type
> The type of a form element. JavaScript 1.1.

value
> The value displayed or submitted by a form element. Nav-
> igator 2; buggy in Internet Explorer 3.

Methods

Input inherits methods from HTMLElement and defines or
overrides the following:

blur()
> Remove keyboard focus from a form element.

click()
> Simulate a mouseclick on a form element.

---

focus()
> Give keyboard focus to a form element.

select()
> Select the text in a form element.

Event Handlers

Input inherits event handlers from HTMLElement and defines or overrides the following:

onblur
> The handler invoked when a form element loses focus.

onchange
> The handler invoked when a form element's value changes.

onclick
> The handler invoked when a form element is clicked. JavaScript 1.0; enhanced in JavaScript 1.1.

onfocus
> The handler invoked when a form element gains focus.

JavaArray   JavaScript representation of a Java array

Availability

Client-side Navigator 3

Synopsis

```
// The length of the array
javaarray.length
// Read or write an array element
javaarray[index]
```

Properties

length
> The number of elements in a Java array.

JavaClass   JavaScript representation of a Java class

Availability

Client-side Navigator 3

Synopsis

```
// Read or write a static Java field or method
javaclass.static_member
// Create a new Java object
new javaclass(...)
```

Properties

Each JavaClass object contains properties that have the same names as the public static fields and methods of the Java class it represents. These properties allow you to read and write the static fields of the class. The properties that represent Java methods refer to JavaMethod objects, which are JavaScript objects that allow you to invoke Java methods. Each JavaClass object has different properties; you can use a for/in loop to enumerate them for any given JavaClass object.

JavaObject   JavaScript representation of a Java object

Availability

Client-side Navigator 3

Synopsis

```
// Read or write an instance field or method
javaobject.member
```

Properties

Each JavaObject object contains properties that have the same names as the public instance fields and methods (but not the static or class fields and methods) of the Java object it represents. These properties allow you to read and write the value of public fields. The properties of a given Java-

---

Object object obviously depend on the type of Java object it represents. You can use the `for/in` loop to enumerate the properties of any given JavaObject.

JavaPackage

JavaScript representation of a Java package

Availability

Client-side Navigator 3

Synopsis

```
// Refers to another JavaPackage
package.package_name
// Refers to a JavaClass object
package.class_name
```

Properties

The properties of a JavaPackage object are the names of the JavaPackage objects and JavaClass objects that it contains. These properties are different for each individual JavaPackage. Note that it is not possible to use the JavaScript `for/in` loop to iterate over the list of property names of a Package object. Consult a Java reference manual to determine the packages and classes contained within any given package.

JSObject

Java representation of a JavaScript object

Availability

A Java class in the *netscape.javascript* package included with Navigator 3 and later

Synopsis

```
public final class netscape.javascript.JSObject
```

Methods

`call(`*`methodName, args[]`*`)`
  Invoke a method of a JavaScript object.

`eval(`*`s`*`)`
  Evaluate a string of JavaScript code.

`getMember(`*`name`*`)`
  Read a property of a JavaScript object.

`getSlot(`*`index`*`)`
  Read an array element of a JavaScript object.

`getWindow(`*`applet`*`)`
  Return initial JSObject for browser window.

`removeMember(`*`name`*`)`
  Delete a property of a JavaScript object.

`setMember(`*`name, value`*`)`
  Set a property of a JavaScript object.

`setSlot(`*`index, value`*`)`
  Set an array element of a JavaScript object.

`toString()`
  Return the string value of a JavaScript object.

Layer   an independent layer in a DHTML document

Availability

Client-side Navigator 4

Synopsis

`document.layers[`*`i`*`]`

Constructor

`new Layer(`*`width, parent`*`)`

Properties

above
  The layer above this one.

background
  The background image of a layer.

below
  The layer below this one.

bgColor
  The background color of a layer.

clip.bottom
  The bottom of the layer's clipping region.

clip.height
  The height of the layer's clipping region.

clip.left
  The left edge of the layer's clipping region.

clip.right
  The right edge of the layer's clipping region.

clip.top
  The top of the layer's clipping region.

clip.width
  The width of the layer's clipping region.

document
  The Document object of a layer.

hidden
  Whether a layer is hidden. Navigator 4; deprecated; use
  Layer.visibility instead.

layers[]
  The layers contained within a layer. Navigator 4; deprecated; use Layer.document.layers instead.

left
  The X-coordinate of a layer.

name
  The name of a layer. Client-side Navigator 4.

---

pageX
> The X-coordinate of a layer, relative to the page.

pageY
> The Y-coordinate of a layer, relative to the page.

parentLayer
> The parent of the layer.

siblingAbove
> The sibling layer above this one.

siblingBelow
> The sibling layer below this one.

src
> The source URL of a layer's content.

top
> The Y-coordinate of a layer.

visibility
> Whether a layer is visible.

window
> The window that contains a layer.

x
> The X-coordinate of a layer.

y
> The Y-coordinate of a layer.

zIndex
> Stacking order of a layer.

Methods

captureEvents(*eventmask*)
> Specify event types to be captured.

handleEvent(*event*)
> Pass an event to the appropriate handler.

load(*src, width*)
> Change layer contents and width.

---

moveAbove(*target*)
  Move one layer above another.

moveBelow(*target*)
  Move one layer below another.

moveBy(*dx, dy*)
  Move a layer to a relative position.

moveTo(*x, y*)
  Move a layer.

moveToAbsolute(*x, y*)
  Move a layer to page coordinates.

offset(*dx, dy*)
  Move a layer to a relative position. Deprecated; use
  Layer.moveBy() instead.

releaseEvents(*eventmask*)
  Stop capturing events.

resizeBy(*dw, dh*)
  Resize a layer by a relative amount.

resizeTo(*width, height*)
  Resize a layer.

routeEvent(*event*)
  Pass a captured event to the next handler.

Link
a hypertext link

Availability

Client-side JavaScript 1.0; enhanced in JavaScript 1.1

Inherits From

HTMLElement

Synopsis

```
document.links[]
document.links.length
```

Properties

Link inherits properties from HTMLElement and also defines or overrides the following:

hash
  The anchor specification of a link.

host
  The hostname and port portions of a link.

hostname
  The hostname portion of a link.

href
  The complete URL of a link.

pathname
  The path portion of a link.

port
  The port portion of a link.

protocol
  The protocol portion of a link.

search
  The query portion of a link.

target
  The target window of a hypertext link.

text
  The text of a link. Navigator 4.

x
  The X-coordinate of a link. Navigator 4.

y
  The Y-coordinate of a link. Navigator 4.

Methods

Link inherits the methods of HTMLElement.

Event Handlers

Link inherits the event handlers of HTMLElement and defines special behavior for the following three:

`onclick`
>   The handler invoked when a link is clicked. JavaScript 1.0; enhanced in JavaScript 1.1.

`onmouseout`
>   The handler invoked when the mouse leaves a link. JavaScript 1.1.

`onmouseover`
>   The handler invoked when the mouse goes over a link.

Location   represents and controls browser location

Availability

Client-side JavaScript 1.0; enhanced in JavaScript 1.1

Synopsis

```
location
window.location
```

Properties

The properties of a Location object refer to the various portions of a URL.

`hash`
>   The anchor specification of the current URL.

`host`
>   The hostname and port portions of the current URL.

`hostname`
>   The hostname portion of the current URL.

`href`
>   The complete currently displayed URL.

`pathname`
>   The path portion of the current URL.

---

port
> The port portion of the current URL.

protocol
> The protocol portion of the current URL.

search
> The query portion of the current URL.

Methods

reload(*force*)
> Reload the current document. JavaScript 1.1.

replace(*url*)
> Replace one displayed document with another. JavaScript 1.1.

Math
> a placeholder for mathematical functions and constants

Availability

Core JavaScript 1.0; ECMA-262

Synopsis

Math.*constant*
Math.*function*()

Constants

Math.E
> The mathematical constant e.

Math.LN10
> The mathematical constant log_e10.

Math.LN2
> The mathematical constant log_e2.

Math.LOG10E
> The mathematical constant $log_{10}e$.

Math.LOG2E
> The mathematical constant log_2e.

```
Math.PI
```
The mathematical constant π.

```
Math.SQRT1_2
```
The mathematical constant $1/\sqrt{2}$.

```
Math.SQRT2
```
The mathematical constant $\sqrt{2}$.

Static Functions

```
Math.abs(x)
```
Compute an absolute value.

```
Math.acos(x)
```
Compute an arc cosine.

```
Math.asin(x)
```
Compute an arc sine.

```
Math.atan(x)
```
Compute an arc tangent.

```
Math.atan2(x, y)
```
Compute the angle from the X-axis to a point.

```
Math.ceil(x)
```
Round a number up.

```
Math.cos(x)
```
Compute a cosine.

```
Math.exp(x)
```
Compute e^x.

```
Math.floor(x)
```
Round a number down.

```
Math.log(x)
```
Compute a natural logarithm.

```
Math.max(a, b)
```
Return the larger of two values.

```
Math.min(a, b)
```
Return the smaller of two values.

```
Math.pow(x, y)
```
Compute x^y.

```
Math.random()
```
Return a pseudo-random number. JavaScript 1.1;
ECMA-262.

```
Math.round(x)
```
Round to the nearest integer.

```
Math.sin(x)
```
Compute a sine.

```
Math.sqrt(x)
```
Compute a square root.

```
Math.tan(x)
```
Compute a tangent.

MimeType   represents a MIME data type

Availability

Client-side Navigator 3

Synopsis

```
navigator.mimeTypes[i]
navigator.mimeTypes["type"]
navigator.mimeTypes.length
```

Properties

description
  A description of a MIME type.

enabledPlugin
  The plugin that handles the MIME type.

suffixes
  Common file suffixes for a MIME type.

type
  The name of a MIME type.

Navigator

information about the browser in use

Availability

Client-side JavaScript 1.0; enhanced in JavaScript 1.1 and 1.2

Synopsis

`navigator`

Properties

`navigator.appCodeName`
The code name of the browser.

`navigator.appName`
The application name of the browser.

`navigator.appVersion`
The platform and version of the browser.

`navigator.language`
The default language of the browser. Navigator 4.

`navigator.mimeTypes[]`
An array of supported MIME types. JavaScript 1.1; always empty in Internet Explorer 4.

`navigator.platform`
The operating system the browser is running under. JavaScript 1.2.

`navigator.plugins[]`
An array of installed plugins. JavaScript 1.1; always empty in Internet Explorer 4.

`navigator.systemLanguage`
The default language of the underlying system. Internet Explorer 4.

`navigator.userAgent`
The HTTP user-agent value.

`navigator.userLanguage`
The language of the current user. Internet Explorer 4.

Functions

`navigator.javaEnabled()`
  Test whether Java is available. JavaScript 1.1.

`navigator.plugins.refresh()`
  Make newly installed plugins available. Navigator 3.

`navigator.preference(prefname, value)`
  Set or retrieve user preferences. Navigator 4; requires
  `UniversalPreferencesRead` privilege to query preferences; requires `UniversalPreferencesWrite` privilege
  to set preference values.

`navigator.savePreferences()`
  Save the user's preferences. Navigator 4; requires
  `UniversalPreferencesWrite` privilege.

`navigator.taintEnabled()`
  Test whether data tainting is enabled. JavaScript 1.1;
  deprecated.

Number   support for numbers

Availability

Core JavaScript 1.1; ECMA-262

Synopsis

`Number.constant`

Constructor

`new Number(value)`
`Number(value)`

Constants

`Number.MAX_VALUE`
  The maximum numeric value.

`Number.MIN_VALUE`
  The minimum numeric value.

Number.NaN
  The special not-a-number value.

Number.NEGATIVE_INFINITY
  Negative infinity.

Number.POSITIVE_INFINITY
  Infinity.

Methods

toString(*radix*)
  Convert a number to a string.

Object

a superclass that contains features of all JavaScript objects

Availability

Core JavaScript 1.0; ECMA-262; enhanced in JavaScript 1.1 and Navigator 4

Constructor

new Object()
new Object(*value*)

Properties

constructor
  An object's constructor function. JavaScript 1.1; ECMA-262.

Methods

assign(*value*)
  Overload the assignment operator. Navigator 3; deprecated in favor of Object.watch().

eval(*code*)
  Evaluate JavaScript code in a string. Navigator 3; deprecated in favor of global eval() function in Navigator 4.

`toString()`
    Define an object's string representation.

`unwatch(propname)`
    Remove a watchpoint. Navigator 4.

`valueOf(typehint)`
    The primitive value of the specified object. JavaScript 1.1;
    ECMA-262.

`watch(propname, handler)`
    Set a watchpoint. Navigator 4.

Option   an option in a Select box

Availability

Client-side JavaScript 1.0; enhanced in JavaScript 1.1

Inherits From

HTMLElement

Synopsis

`select.options[i]`

Properties

Option inherits the properties of HTMLElement and also
defines the following:

`defaultSelected`
    Whether an object is selected by default.

`index`
    The position of the option.

`selected`
    Whether the option is selected.

`text`
    The label for an option. JavaScript 1.0; read/write in
    JavaScript 1.1.

---

value
> The value returned when the form is submitted.

Password

a text input field for sensitive data

Availability

Client-side JavaScript 1.0; enhanced in JavaScript 1.1

Inherits From

Input, HTMLElement

Synopsis

```
form.name
form.elements[i]
```

Properties

Password inherits properties from Input and HTMLElement
and defines or overrides the following:

value
> User input to the Password object. JavaScript 1.0;
> modified in JavaScript 1.2.

Methods

Password inherits methods from Input and HTMLElement.

Event Handlers

Password inherits methods from Input and HTMLElement.

Plugin

describes an installed plugin

Availability

Client-side Navigator 3

Synopsis

```
navigator.plugins[i]
navigator.plugins['name']
```

Properties

description
> English description of a plugin.

filename
> The filename of the plugin program.

length
> The number of MIME types supported.

name
> The name of a plugin.

PrivilegeManager
Java class used by signed scripts

Availability

Client-side Navigator 4

Synopsis

```
netscape.security.PrivilegeManager
```

Methods

disablePrivilege(privilege)
> Disable a privilege.

enablePrivilege(privilege)
> Enable a privilege.

Radio
a graphical radio button

Availability

Client-side JavaScript 1.0; enhanced in JavaScript 1.1

Inherits From

Input, HTMLElement

Synopsis

```
// A group of radio buttons with the same name
form.name[i]
```

Properties

Radio inherits properties from Input and HTMLElement, and defines or overrides the following:

checked
> Whether a Radio button is selected.

defaultChecked
> Initial state of a Radio button.

value
> Value returned when form is submitted.

Methods

Radio inherits methods from Input and HTMLElement.

Event Handlers

Radio inherits event handlers from Input and HTMLElement and defines or overrides the following:

onclick
> The handler invoked when a Radio button is selected.

RegExp   regular expressions for pattern matching

Availability

Core JavaScript 1.2

Constructor

```
new RegExp(pattern, attributes)
```

Instance Properties

global
> Whether a regular expression matches globally. Not implemented in IE 4.

ignoreCase
> Whether a regular expression is case-insensitive. Not implemented in IE 4.

lastIndex
> The character position after the last match. Not implemented in IE 4.

source
> The text of the regular expression.

Static Properties

RegExp.$*n*
> The text that matched the *n*th subexpression.

RegExp.input or RegExp.$_
> The input buffer for pattern matching. Non-functional in IE 4.

RegExp.lastMatch or RegExp["$&"]
> The text of the last successful pattern match. Not implemented in IE 4.

RegExp.lastParen or RegExp["$+"]
> The text that matched the last subexpression. Not implemented in IE 4.

RegExp.leftContext or RegExp["$`"]
> The text before the last match. Not implemented in IE 4.

RegExp.multiline or RegExp["$*"]
> Whether matches are performed in multi-line mode. Not implemented in IE 4.

RegExp.rightContext or RegExp["$'"]
> The text after the last match. Not implemented in IE 4.

Methods

compile(*newpattern, attributes*)
 Change a regular expression.

exec(*string*)
 General-purpose pattern matching. Buggy in IE 4.

test(*string*)
 Test whether a string contains a match.

Reset   a button to reset a form's values

Availability

Client-side JavaScript 1.0; enhanced in JavaScript 1.1

Inherits From

Input, HTMLElement

Synopsis

form.*name*
form.elements[*i*]

Properties

Reset inherits properties from Input and HTMLElement and
defines or overrides the following:

value
 The label of a Reset button.

Methods

Reset inherits the methods of Input and HTMLElement.

Event Handlers

Reset inherits the event handlers of Input and HTMLElement
and defines or overrides the following:

---

onclick
>   The handler invoked when a Reset button is clicked.
>   JavaScript 1.0; enhanced in JavaScript 1.1.

Screen   provides information about the display

Availability

Client-side JavaScript 1.2

Synopsis

screen

Properties

screen.availHeight
>   The available height of the screen.

screen.availLeft
>   The first available horizontal pixel. Navigator 4.

screen.availTop
>   The first available vertical pixel. Navigator 4.

screen.availWidth
>   The available width of the screen.

screen.colorDepth
>   The depth of the web browser's color palette.

screen.height
>   The height of the screen.

screen.pixelDepth
>   The color depth of the screen. Navigator 4.

screen.width
>   The width of the screen.

Select

a graphical selection list

Availability

Client-side JavaScript 1.0; enhanced in JavaScript 1.1

Inherits From

Input, HTMLElement

Synopsis

```
form.element_name
form.elements[i]
```

Properties

Select inherits properties from Input and HTMLElement and defines or overrides the following:

length
>   The number of options in a Select object.

options[]
>   The choices in a Select object. JavaScript 1.0; enhanced in JavaScript 1.1.

selectedIndex
>   The selected option. JavaScript 1.0; writeable in JavaScript 1.1.

type
>   Type of form element. JavaScript 1.1.

Methods

Select inherits the methods of Input and HTMLElement.

Event Handlers

Select inherits event handlers from Input and HTMLElement and defines or overrides the following:

onchange
>   The handler invoked when the selection changes.

String   support for strings

Availability

Core JavaScript 1.0; enhanced in Navigator 3

Constructor

```
new String(value)      // JavaScript 1.1
```

Properties

length
   The length of a string. JavaScript 1.0; ECMA-262.

Methods

anchor(name)
   Add an HTML anchor to a string.

big()
   Make a string <BIG>.

blink()
   Make a string <BLINK>.

bold()
   Make a string bold with <B>.

charAt(n)
   Get the nth character from a string. JavaScript 1.0; ECMA-
   262.

charCodeAt(n)
   Get the nth character code from a string. JavaScript 1.2;
   ECMA-262.

concat(value,...)
   Concatenate strings. JavaScript 1.2.

fixed()
   Make a string fixed-width with <TT>.

fontcolor(color)
   Set a string's color with <FONT>.

fontsize(*size*)
  Set a string's font size with <FONT>.

indexOf(*substring, start*)
  Search a string. JavaScript 1.0; ECMA-262.

italics()
  Make a string italic with <I>.

lastIndexOf(*substring, start*)
  Search a string backwards. JavaScript 1.0; ECMA-262.

link(*href*)
  Add a hypertext link to a string.

match(*regexp*)
  Find one or more regular expression matches. JavaScript 1.2.

replace*regexp, replacement*)
  Replace substring(s) matching a regular expression. JavaScript 1.2.

search(*regexp*)
  Search for a regular expression. JavaScript 1.2.

slice(*start, end*)
  Extract a substring. JavaScript 1.2.

small()
  Make a string <SMALL>.

split(*delimiter*)
  Break a string into an array of strings. JavaScript 1.1; ECMA-262.

strike()
  Strike out a string with <STRIKE>.

sub()
  Make a string a subscript with <SUB>.

substring(*from, to*)
  Return a substring of a string. JavaScript 1.0; ECMA-262.

substr(*start, length*)
  Extract a substring. JavaScript 1.2.

```
sup()
```
Make a string a superscript with <SUP>.

```
toLowerCase()
```
Convert a string to lowercase. JavaScript 1.0; ECMA-262.

```
toUpperCase()
```
Convert a string to uppercase. JavaScript 1.0; ECMA-262.

Static Methods

```
String.fromCharCode(c1, c2, ...)
```
Create a string from character encodings. JavaScript 1.2; ECMA-262.

Style   cascading style sheet attributes

Availability

Client-side JavaScript 1.2

Synopsis

```
// Navigator
document.classes.className.tagName
document.ids.elementName
document.tags.tagName
document.contextual(...)

// Internet Explorer
htmlElement.style
```

Properties

The Style object has properties corresponding to each of the CSS attributes supported by the browser.

Methods

```
borderWidths(top, right, bottom, left)
```
Set all border width properties. Navigator 4.

---

margins(*top*, *right*, *bottom*, *left*)
    Set all margin properties. Navigator 4.

paddings(*top*, *right*, *bottom*, *left*)
    Set all padding properties. Navigator 4.

Submit

a button to submit a form

Availability

Client-side JavaScript 1.0; enhanced in JavaScript 1.1

Inherits From

Input, HTMLElement

Synopsis

```
form.name
form.elements[i]
```

Properties

Submit inherits properties from Input and HTMLElement and defines or overrides the following:

value
    The label of a Submit button.

Methods

Submit inherits the methods from Input and HTMLElement.

Event Handlers

Submit inherits event handlers from Input and HTMLElement and defines or overrides the following:

onclick
    Invoked when a Submit button is clicked. JavaScript 1.0; enhanced in JavaScript 1.1.

Text
a graphical text input field

Availability

Client-side JavaScript 1.0; enhanced in JavaScript 1.1

Inherits From

Input, HTMLElement

Synopsis

```
form.name
form.elements[i]
```

Properties

Text inherits properties from Input and HTMLElement and defines or overrides the following:

value
  User input to the Text object.

Methods

Text inherits the methods of Input and HTMLElement.

Event Handlers

Text inherits the event handlers of Input and HTMLElement and defines or overrides the following:

onchange
  The handler invoked when input value changes.

Textarea
a multiline text input area

Availability

Client-side JavaScript 1.0; enhanced in JavaScript 1.1

Inherits From

Input, HTMLElement

Synopsis

```
form.name
form.elements[i]
```

Properties

Textarea inherits the properties of Input and HTMLElement and defines or overrides the following:

value
  User input to the Textarea object.

Methods

Textarea inherits the methods of Input and HTMLElement.

Event Handlers

Textarea inherits the event handlers of Input and HTMLElement and defines or overrides the following:

onchange
  The handler invoked when input value changes.

URL   see Link, Location, or Document.URL

Window   a web browser window or frame

Availability

Client-side JavaScript 1.0; enhanced in JavaScript 1.1 and 1.2

Synopsis

```
self
window
window.frames[i]
```

Properties

The Window object defines the following properties. Non-portable, browser-specific properties are listed separately after this list:

---

closed
> Whether a window has been closed. JavaScript 1.1.

defaultStatus
> The default status line text.

document
> The Document of the window.

frames[]
> List of frames within a window.

history
> The History of the window.

length
> The number of frames in the window.

location
> The URL of the window.

name
> The name of a window. JavaScript 1.0; read/write in JavaScript 1.1.

navigator
> A reference to the Navigator object.

offscreenBuffering
> Whether window updates are buffered. JavaScript 1.2.

opener
> The window that opened this one. JavaScript 1.1.

parent
> The parent of a frame.

screen
> Information about the screen. JavaScript 1.2.

self
> The window itself.

status
> Specify a transient status-line message.

top
> The window of a frame.

---

window
> The window itself.

Navigator Properties

crypto
> Reference to the Crypto object. Navigator 4.04 and later.

innerHeight
> The height of the document display area. Navigator 4; UniversalBrowserWrite privilege required to set to less than 100 pixels.

innerWidth
> The width of the document display area. Navigator 4; UniversalBrowserWrite privilege required to set to less than 100 pixels.

java
> The *java.** LiveConnect package. Navigator 3.

locationbar
> The visibility of the browser's location bar. Navigator 4; UniversalBrowserWrite privilege required to change visibility.

menubar
> The visibility of the browser's menubar. Navigator 4; UniversalBrowserWrite privilege required to change visibility.

netscape
> The *netscape.** LiveConnect Java package. Navigator 3.

outerHeight
> The height of the window area. Navigator 4; UniversalBrowserWrite privilege required to set to less than 100 pixels.

outerWidth
> The width of the window. Navigator 4; UniversalBrowserWrite privilege required to set to less than 100 pixels.

Packages
  LiveConnect packages of Java classes. Navigator 3.

pageXOffset
  The current horizontal scroll position. Navigator 4.

pageYOffset
  The current vertical scroll position. Navigator 4.

personalbar
  The visibility of the browser's personal bar. Navigator 4;
  UniversalBrowserWrite privilege required to change
  visibility.

screenX
  The X-coordinate of a window on the screen. Navigator 4.

screenY
  The Y-coordinate of a window on the screen. Navigator 4.

scrollbars
  The visibility of the browser's scroll bars. Navigator 4;
  UniversalBrowserWrite privilege required to change
  visibility.

statusbar
  The visibility of the browser's status line. Navigator 4;
  UniversalBrowserWrite privilege required to change
  visibility.

sun
  The *sun.** LiveConnect Java package. Navigator 3.

toolbar
  The visibility of the browser's toolbar. Navigator 4;
  UniversalBrowserWrite privilege required to change
  visibility.

Internet Explorer Properties

clientInformation
  Synonym for Window.navigator. Internet Explorer 4.

event
  Describes the most recent event. Internet Explorer 4.

Methods

The Window object has the following portable methods. Non-portable, browser-specific methods are listed after this list.

alert(*message*)
> Display a message in a dialog box.

blur()
> Remove keyboard focus from a top-level window. JavaScript 1.1.

clearInterval(*intervalId*)
> Stop periodically executing code. JavaScript 1.2.

clearTimeout(*timeoutId*)
> Cancel deferred execution.

close()
> Close a browser window.

confirm(*question*)
> Ask a yes-or-no question.

focus()
> Give keyboard focus to a top-level window. JavaScript 1.1.

moveBy(*dx, dy*)
> Move a window to a relative position. JavaScript 1.2; Navigator 4 requires UniversalBrowserWrite privilege to move the window off-screen.

moveTo(*x, y*)
> Move a window to an absolute position. JavaScript 1.2; Navigator 4 requires UniversalBrowserWrite privilege to move the window off-screen.

open(*url, name, features, replace*)
> Open a new browser window or locate a named window. JavaScript 1.0; enhanced in JavaScript 1.1.

prompt(*message, default*)
> Get string input in a dialog.

`resizeBy(`*dw*`,` *dh*`)`

    Resize a window by a relative amount. JavaScript 1.2;
    Navigator 4 requires `UniversalBrowserWrite` privilege
    to set either width or height to less than 100 pixels.

`resizeTo(`*width,* *height*`)`

    Resize a window. JavaScript 1.2; Navigator 4 requires
    `UniversalBrowserWrite` privilege to set either width or
    height to less than 100 pixels.

`scroll(`*x,* *y*`)`

    Scroll a document in a window. JavaScript 1.1; deprecated
    in JavaScript 1.2 in favor of `scrollTo()`.

`scrollBy(`*dx,* *dy*`)`

    Scroll the document by a relative amount. JavaScript 1.2.

`scrollTo(`*x,* *y*`)`

    Scroll the document. JavaScript 1.2.

`setInterval(`*code,* *interval*`)`
`setInterval(`*func,* *interval,* *args*`...)`

    Periodically execute specified code. JavaScript 1.2;
    Internet Explorer 4 supports only the first form of
    this method.

`setTimeout(`*code,* *delay*`)`

    Defer execution of code.

Navigator 4 Methods

`atob(`*str64*`)`

    Decode base-64 encoded data.

`back()`

    Go back to previous document.

`btoa(`*data*`)`

    Encode binary data using base-64 ASCII encoding.

`captureEvents(`*eventmask*`)`

    Specify event types to be captured.

`disableExternalCapture()`

    Disable cross-server event capturing. Requires
    `UniversalBrowserWrite` privilege.

enableExternalCapture()
    Enable cross-server event capturing. Requires
    UniversalBrowserWrite privilege.

find(*target, caseSensitive, backwards*)
    Search the document.

forward()
    Go forward to next document.

handleEvent(*event*)
    Pass an event to the appropriate handler.

home()
    Display the home page.

print()
    Print the document.

releaseEvents(*eventmask*)
    Stop capturing events.

routeEvent(*event*)
    Pass a captured event to the next handler.

setHotkeys(*enabled*)
    Allow or disallow keyboard shortcuts. Requires
    UniversalBrowserWrite privilege.

setResizable(*resizable*)
    Allow or disallow window resizing. Requires
    UniversalBrowserWrite privilege.

setZOptions(*option*)
    Control window stacking. Requires
    UniversalBrowserWrite privilege.

stop()
    Stop loading the document.

Internet Explorer Methods

navigate(*url*)
    Load a new URL. Internet Explorer 3.

Event Handlers

onblur

> The handler invoked when the window loses keyboard focus. JavaScript 1.1.

ondragdrop

> The handler invoked when the user drops items in the window. Navigator 4.

onerror

> The handler invoked when a JavaScript error occurs. JavaScript 1.1.

onfocus

> Invoked when window is given focus. JavaScript 1.1.

onload

> The handler invoked when a document finishes loading.

onmove

> The handler invoked when a window is moved. Navigator 4; not supported on Navigator 4 Unix platforms.

onresize

> The handler invoked when a window is resized. JavaScript 1.2.

onunload

> The handler invoked when the browser leaves a page.